Don't Let Your

Money

Kick The Bucket

Before You Do

Don’t Let Your Money Kick The Bucket Before You Do

ISBN: 978-0-9861398-0-2

Printed in the United States of America

Book interior and book cover design by Jean Boles
jean.bolesbooks@gmail.com
https://www.upwork.com/fl/jeanboles

Don't Let Your MONEY Kick the Bucket Before You Do!

www.bettermoneydecisions.com
(844) 507-0961

Kate Stalter

TABLE OF CONTENTS

Foreword

"In this book, I offer insights gleaned from years of working with clients to develop successful retirement strategies using all the available resources."

Back in the era of rich corporate pensions and shorter life expectancy, there wasn't much need for financial planning. Many retirees had guaranteed income, and they weren't responsible for salting it away themselves.

Meanwhile, people only lived a few years in retirement, and were frequently in poor health. There wasn't much golfing or exotic world travel for the 1950s-era retiree.

The wealthy had estate planning. But for the middle class — people who had been employees or small-business owners — there wasn't any reason to do much financial planning other than a household budget.

Although people tend to feel nostalgia for bygone eras, believing everything was "better" in the past, that's simply not true. Small business owners and farmers didn't have pensions or retirement accounts, and many worked until their dying day. Medical advancements mean people live long and healthy lives, even after experiencing a condition or event that would have killed them just a few decades ago.

But there's a catch: You don't want to outlive your money.

That's where having a plan comes in. Rather than being a rulebook, a financial plan is part cold, hard truth and part "what if" exercise. What if you worked a little longer? What if you saved more before you retired? What if you waited a little longer to claim Social Security? What if you engineered your portfolio to deliver the return you require to maintain your lifestyle, while lowering risk, so a severe market correction wouldn't decimate you?

Running those scenarios requires sophisticated software. That's another reason why the pre-boomer generations didn't plan; the technology simply didn't exist.

But emotions play into the planning process even more than technology. Nobody is "perfect" when it comes to their finances. The majority of people make mistakes with their money. However, when Wall Street brokers run commercials of well-coifed older couples holding hands on the beach, Main Street investors feel inadequate.

Come on. Does anybody really look and act like the models in the brokers' commercials?

The financial media compound the problem. The financial TV channels run fast-paced coverage of every market movement, asking pundits how the audience should "play" the news item du jour. Others come on and discuss "reading the tea leaves" of the Federal Reserve or the Bank of Japan or the employment report.

Meanwhile, financial magazines have their own lists of "must-buy" stocks or tax tips or best places to retire. Ever notice that those places are different every year?

"My chief goal is to open your eyes to the potentially dire consequences of poor financial decisions."

That's because it's all entertainment. It's not financial advice. It's not a plan for you.

Often, it's not even good information. It's certainly not tailored to your unique situation.

Today's cacophony of financial chatter actually makes it difficult for people to figure out what information is valuable, and which is just noise.

I've seen people give up because it's all overwhelming. In addition, most of us have some sort of "confirmation bias." We gravitate toward that which validates our existing opinions or assumptions. That's behind the success of many financial media outlets.

Don't agree with one pundit? Just keep watching that market channel or click on the next link. Somebody else will be along shortly, and you'll like what he or she is saying.

Again, none of this is financial planning. Imagine going into your kitchen to make dinner, and you see some ingredients you like. Maybe some chicken in the fridge. But there's also coconut water. You spot some strawberries. In the pantry, you have cayenne pepper and whole-wheat flour.

On their own, there's nothing wrong with these ingredients. But unless you're a contestant on *Chopped*, good luck using them to form a cohesive dish.

There would have been other approaches to this kitchen scenario. You could have figured out what you wanted for dinner and determined whether you needed to shop for ingredients. Or you could have taken a more thoughtful approach to the ingredients at hand and been more deliberate in choosing items that would work well together to compose a dish.

You get the point. Money is, of course, a much more emotional issue. In this day and age, for people who have worked and saved or who have a pension, there's no downside to doing some kind of plan, even if it's simple and streamlined.

One of the common mistakes I see involves people underestimating their retirement expenses or under-estimating how long they may live. A plan doesn't always deliver news that people want to hear, but it is a good place to begin understanding the scenarios you may face, and to give you some ways to create a better future for yourself and your family.

For the Boomer generation, retirement is a much more difficult puzzle to solve than it was for their parents.

In this book, I offer insights gleaned from years of working with clients to develop successful retirement strategies using all the available resources — investments, Social Security and other assets. Rather than using the traditional bone-dry ways of discussing finance, I endeavored to make these chapters fun and accessible.

My chief goal is to open your eyes to the potentially dire consequences of poor financial decisions. But I also offer real strategies for creating the retirement you dream of.

This book is for you.

1

Retirement Planning

Rethinking Retirement At 65

"How will you pay for your expenses in your retirement years? Don't assume that expenses will decline."

Ask Americans what age they associate with retirement and one number comes up repeatedly: 65. Time to quit toiling for a paycheck and enjoy time with family, travel and activities you couldn't squeeze in while you were working.

But is that necessarily a good idea? How did the retirement age of 65 become so firmly implanted in the popular psyche?

Part of it is likely because the Medicare age remains 65, although the full Social Security retirement age has crept up over the years.

That deeply ingrained age of 65 has its origins in Germany, when 65 was instituted as the official retirement age in 1916.

When Social Security was introduced in 1935, it specified 65 as the full retirement age. Private-sector companies were gravitating toward that age as well.

This number became fixed in Americans' minds. Let's put this in some context: In 1935, the average U.S. life expectancy was about 60 for men and 64 for women. In other words, an American had about a 50-50 chance of living to 65.

Flash forward eight decades. According to the World Health Organization, the overall average life expectancy in the U.S. had grown to 79 by 2013.

Here's where we should start questioning the wisdom of retiring at 65.

- Not only is the average life expectancy rising, but the number of Americans living to 100 is growing fast. According to a 2015 report from the Centers for Disease Control and Prevention, the number of U.S. centenarians grew by 43 percent between 2000 and 2014.[1]

---

[1] More Americans are living past their 100th birthdays: http://www.cbsnews.com/news/more-americans-are-living-past-their-100th-birthdays/

- Americans simply are not saving enough to sustain lengthy retirements: According to the Government Accountability Office, the median account value for Americans who have savings is about $104,000 for households headed by a person between 55 and 64. That number rises a little for households headed by a person between 65 and 74, to $148,000.[2] That's equivalent to an inflation-protected annuity of $310 and $649 per month, respectively. Even with the addition of a Social Security check, that's hardly enough to sustain a typical middle-class lifestyle.

- Social Security provides most of the income for about half of American households age 65 and older. The average monthly Social Security retirement benefit, as of January, was $1,341.[3] Again, this is not enough to cover the typical expenses for many Americans.

There's an ongoing debate about whether genetics or lifestyle contribute more to longevity. I'm no scientist — I don't even play one on TV. But the rapid growth of the over-100 population in the U.S., along with rising life expectancies, seems to suggest that medical advances, combined with major lifestyle shifts, such as use of seat belts and avoidance of cigarettes, is contributing to our longevity.

---

[2] Most Households Approaching Retirement Have Low Savings: http://www.gao.gov/assets/680/670153.pdf

[3] What is the average monthly benefit for a retired worker? https://faq.ssa.gov/link/portal/34011/34019/Article/3736/What-is-the-average-monthly-benefit-for-a-retired-worker

How will you pay for your expenses in your retirement years? Don't assume that expenses will decline. For years, there has been a "rule of thumb" that retirees should count on expenses of 70 percent to 80 percent of their preretirement level. Planning software (designed by younger people) even began to incorporate that assumption.

But there are a couple things wrong with that assumption. First, healthy retirees aren't interested in downsizing their lifestyle. On the contrary, people want to travel and engage in long-neglected hobbies. As people age, medical spending grows and travel spending declines. In other words, you'll always be spending money on wants or needs.

"It sounds great to kick back and relax, but how relaxing does it sound to run out of money a few years after retirement?"

Circling back to the increased U.S. longevity, there's another, more sobering way to view that old saw about decreased retirement spending: If you retire in your 60s with a small amount in savings, your nest egg might not sustain you for another 25, 30 or even 35 years. In that scenario, you have no choice but to slash spending.

Decades ago, with shorter life expectancies, people could better afford to retire at 65. These days, Americans face the very real possibility of outliving their money.

What's the solution? It's probably not one thing, but a combination. If you are still working, consider saving more. Review your spending. Are there places you can cut back?

Also look at your financial resources. Consider consolidating accounts, and be sure your investments are allocated in an efficient manner. A heavy concentration in single stocks is risky and can have serious negative effects. Do you know the expected return of your investments and how much income your portfolio should generate and for how long?

The conventional wisdom about a carefree retirement at 65 no longer applies to everyone. It sounds great to kick back and relax, but how relaxing does it sound to run out of money a few years after retirement?

2

Don't Kid Yourself: You Can't Work Forever

"My grandparents' generation had something that's become increasingly rare: The fully funded pension."

"I'll never retire. I love what I do!"

Have you ever said that? If you haven't said it yourself, then I'm sure you've heard it from others.

The idea that people won't retire seems to have gained popularity with the baby boom generation. After all, in the 1965 song "My Generation," The Who famously sang, "Hope I die before I get old." Roger Daltrey was around 21 at the time; he's 72 now. Pete Townshend would have been 20 in 1965; he's 71 now. Consider this: If Mr. Daltrey and Mr. Townshend were U.S. citizens, they would both be taking Social Security!

I understand where the anti-retirement mindset comes from. When I was a teenager, I went on family trips to visit grandparents in Naples, Fla., a magnet for retirees, then and now.

"It's imperative that you plan for a day when you will no longer have a paycheck to finance your life."

All four of my grandparents were born between 1908 and 1913. For that generation, retirement really did mean shuffleboard, bingo games, Lawrence Welk, and many of the interests and activities that are treated as comedic punchlines today. I was bored when I went down to Florida to see the grandparents. And I don't think I was the only kid in that era who got a bad impression of retirement. To this day, comedians can still get a laugh with references to retirees.

But my grandparents' generation had something that's become increasingly rare: The fully funded pension. That, along with Social Security, afforded a secure, enjoyable retirement for many.

As we know, the days of the luxurious pension are all but gone — for private sector employees, anyway. Even government employees are seeing their pension benefits cut.

So there's no question that retirement is a very different proposition today than it was in the 1970s and 1980s. Two different social trends are colliding.

"A growing body of research is showing that people have a hard time imagining themselves in the future."

– From Harvard psychology professor Daniel Gilbert's book, *Stumbling on Happiness*

First, the pension has fallen by the wayside, and we are now responsible for funding our own retirements. You may not like it, you may blame somebody — for example, greedy corporations or a particular political party — but ultimately, you still have to face that reality. Pointing fingers won't grow your bank balance.

Second, thanks to tremendous advances in medical science, along with healthier lifestyles, we are living longer. A 65-year-old in the United States has a greater-than-average chance of living to his or her mid-80s.[4] It's also increasingly common to see people living until their 90s or even 100.

And please, please don't say, "My parents only lived to age 60." These days, lifestyle and medical science are keeping people alive — and active — longer than in previous generations. That means most of us will have to fund many years of our lives without a paycheck from work. But here's

---

[4] How much longer might you live? Think again http://www.cbsnews.com/news/two-common-mistakes-we-make-thinking-about-how-long-we-might-live/

where things get dicey, and where people like to jump in with the refrain of, "I'll never retire. I love what I do."

I hate to be the bearer of bad news, but the reality is: No matter how much you love what you do, the majority of people slow down by their mid-70s. We can all cite anecdotal examples of people who keep working; I'm not interested in that.

The Warren Buffetts and Betty Whites of the world — octogenarians and nonagenarians who are still going strong in their careers — are very rare. It's also not unusual to see business owners who go into work every day, well into their 80s. But if you drill down, you'll find that it's often because the owner is either a control freak or doesn't know what else to do with himself.

I work with a lot of people around the northern part of the state, doing retirement planning. I know of very few people who keep a fully active, working schedule through age 80.

"Are you stashing your money under the mattress, where it has no chance of keeping up with inflation?"

On the other hand, I know an inordinate number of people who seem to believe they can just keep financing their lives through work until the day they die.

Keep in mind that I'm not talking about people with an active schedule of volunteer work or perhaps hobbies they monetize, or even some consulting work here and there. No, that's entirely different from people who are forced to work at age 80 just to keep a roof over their heads.

Please don't kid yourself that you won't live long enough to worry about retirement. And don't kid yourself that you will feel like working until the very end.

Maybe you never plan on moving to Florida, wearing pastels and taking up golf. But it's imperative that you plan for a day when you will no longer have a paycheck to finance your life.

Be wary of doomsday scenarios trumpeted in media

We face plenty of impediments when trying to envision our future selves. Behavioral issues are some of the biggest hurdles. In other words, our own beliefs and biases get in the way of sound financial decisions.

It's very fashionable these days to have a negative and cynical outlook on — well, pretty much everything, it seems. Arguing with strangers on social media has become a national pastime. The relative anonymity means people feel free to sling snarks and insults they would never utter in a face-to-face conversation.

And if you watch cable news channels, you're regularly treated to red-faced commentators shouting at each other over some issue of the day. Who knows whether it's actually important? The network was able to find people willing to have a heated disagreement on-screen.

It reminds me of Chicken Little from the old story. After getting hit with an acorn, he ran around screaming, "The sky is falling!" If you recall, it wasn't too difficult to get the other animals to join him in proclaiming that doomsday was nigh.

Now, please don't misunderstand. I'm not suggesting that we shouldn't be prepared for bad things to happen. In fact, I advocate planning for retirement and other life events, such as health care issues, that have a reasonable chance of happening at some future date.

However, that preparation can be thwarted by our own financial blind spots, and, let's face it, by a widespread idea that cynicism is a more valid outlook than optimism.

"The best way to hedge against risk of "doomsday scenarios" is by maintaining a balanced, globally diversified portfolio."

When it comes to our finances, that confirmation bias kicks in when we seek out or favor information that confirms our existing beliefs and opinions. You think the entire global stock market will come crashing down for some reason? You can find confirmation for this, which provides further confirmation that you are correct in stashing your money under the mattress, where it has no chance of keeping up with inflation.

But here's the thing: The Chicken Littles didn't arrive on the scene in the past five years. They've always been here. If you look back at media predictions going back to the 1970s (as good a starting point as any), you'll see some spectacularly wrong calls, based on pessimism. If these were simple media goofs, they would be humorous in hindsight. However, people undoubtedly made financial decisions based on some, if not all, of these erroneous predictions.

- Time magazine, Sept. 9, 1974: "A Gallup poll published last month found that 46 percent of adults feared a depression similar to the classic one of the 1930s."[5]

- Business Week, Aug. 13, 1979: Cover story, "The Death of Equities." An excerpt from the article: "The old attitude of buying solid stocks as a cornerstone for one's life savings and retirement has simply disappeared. ... The death of equities is a near permanent condition." [6]

- Forbes, July 19, 1993: Cover story, "Bearish on America." Morgan Stanley's Barton Biggs advised readers to sell U.S. stocks, saying Bill Clinton's policies were bad for America. In fact, the S&P 500 index delivered a compound return of 18.5 percent over the next seven years.[7]

- Fortune magazine, Sept. 28, 1998: Cover story, "The Crash of '98: Can The U.S. Economy Hold Up?" Columnist Joseph Nocera wrote, "This time it is different. This time the market won't be so quick to bounce back ... Who can look at the world and not conclude that things have changed dramatically?" [8]

---

[5] http://kickthebucketbook.com/resources/

[6] Business Week's "The Death of Equities" Revisited: http://www.fiendbear.com/deatheq.htm

[7] Barton Biggs, Erudite Wordsmith Of Global Finance http://www.forbes.com/sites/robertlenzner/2012/07/16/barton-biggs-colorful-troubador-of-the-stock-market/#419351e55105

[8] Eyes on the Press: Fortune - Requiem for a Bear, or a Tale of MisFortune? http://www.fool.com/Specials/1999/sp990121EyeOnPress002.htm

(Hat tip to Weston Wellington of Dimensional Fund Advisors, who gathered some of these examples, along with many others.)

Of course, with all of these headlines, we have the benefit of hindsight to know how wrong they were. So it's not really about having a good laugh at someone else's expense. The point here is that dire predictions don't necessarily become reality.

"The approach you take to the reality of market downturns can have a big effect on your retirement."

However, because people often want their pessimistic biases confirmed, headlines like these are magnets for those with an existing belief that untold destruction is just around the corner. That bias can and does result in lost investment opportunity, as well as panic-driven decisions to buy something perceived as a "safe" investment.

Rather than being an argument against remaining invested, an analysis of these headlines reveals that the pundits simply don't know what will happen in the future. Our emotions aren't the best way to gauge future events, either. The best way to hedge against risk of "doomsday scenarios" is by maintaining a balanced, globally diversified portfolio. That way, you account for everyone's predictions, both negative and positive, as well as for the events that no one ever predicted!

Retirement factors to consider beyond stock market

The stock market volatility in early 2016 certainly grabbed investors' attention. Whether or not you believe the worst is behind us or still to come, the relentless focus on market action obscures the importance of many other crucial financial-planning steps.

In the long run, decisions about investment withdrawals, day-to-day spending and even Social Security claiming strategies typically have a greater effect on your well-being than whatever the market does over the next days, weeks and months.

Here are some financial considerations that don't have the same excitement factor as tracking market action, but tend to be more important.

- **Estimating retirement expenses:** Forget the old trope about expenses declining in retirement. That's usually true, but not because you're spending less on work clothes, lunches or commuting. Most people spend less in retirement because they have no choice. They don't have a paycheck from work anymore, and can't spend as freely. Most people don't like slashing their lifestyle, but sadly, it's often necessary.

  Also, people often underestimate the effect of taxes in retirement. Even many advisers are unaware of the impact, and simply revert to so-called "conventional wisdom" that taxes are not a significant post-retirement concern. The reality is that income from Social Security, required minimum distributions from retirement accounts and other sources is considered taxable. That can mean a bigger financial hit than you had anticipated.

- **Planning for longevity:** Nearly every retiree receives Social Security, based upon his or her own work history or a spouse's.

  But people often think about Social Security the wrong way, believing they should grab the money at age 62, the moment it becomes available. That incorrect thinking is based on something called the "break-even analysis," which shows the age at which the decision to delay benefits pays off, relative to taking the money early.

  However, Social Security is best viewed as insurance against living too long. That's not always an easy concept to grasp, given that life insurance is typically used to protect against early death. By delaying the Social Security benefit, you increase your income flow as you age. If you take the money at age 62, you don't receive the full benefit to which you are entitled. In addition, your benefit remains low for the rest of your life. In other words, money in your pocket today could mean less money 25 or 30 years from now.

- **Anticipating poor market conditions in retirement:** For today's retirees, who lived through the market decline of 2000 and then the debacle of 2008, it doesn't require a big stretch of the imagination to envision a poor market.

However, the approach you take to the reality of market downturns can have a big effect on your retirement.

It's perfectly understandable to look for "safe" assets to cushion your nest egg. Cash, gold and bonds are some of the most common instruments that people turn to when hoping to avoid a market roller coaster ride.

Unfortunately, cash doesn't keep up with inflation over time, gold is volatile in the short-term and has not been a proven long-term investment, and bonds should be used to dampen the volatility of stocks, rather than being held primarily for income. In addition, people holding long-term bonds, believing they are "safe," might suffer at some point in the future, if interest rates do begin rising more than 25 basis points at a time.

In other words, cash, gold and bonds are not the best ways to mitigate stock market choppiness. While that might sound like bad news, it's actually not. There are better ways to invest for growth, while still protecting yourself against the downside, particularly in the early years of retirement.

Recent research indicates that poor market conditions during those first few years can have particularly harmful effects.[9] That's because recent

---

[9] Ready To Retire? When planning for income, consider how the sequence of returns could impact a portfolio's value over time https://www.mfs.com/wps/FileServerServlet?articleId=templatedata/internet/file/data/sales_tools/mfsp_classeq_sfl&servletCommand=default

retirees are pulling out money while markets are trading at lows. That makes it more difficult for a portfolio to rally back and deliver the required returns.

It's possible, however, to mitigate this problem, known as sequence-of-returns risk. To weather downward-trending markets, investors must be aware of their withdrawal rates. In addition, holding a balanced stock-and-bond portfolio, and separating out the assets you will need in the short term, can help you avoid the ugly consequences of selling investments during market declines.

"There are some exceptions, but in most cases, account owners are well advised to move their 401(k) accounts out of a former employer's program."

These are three areas where people can take some steps to shore up their retirement income and assets, while reducing the effects of day-to-day market swings, or even years of sharp market declines.

Don't forget retirement accounts at former employers

Most people wouldn't admit to forgetting about their own money, or even leaving their money in a place where it's unsupervised and left to its own devices.

Unfortunately, there are plenty of "orphaned" 401(k) accounts, just lying around in various brokerages throughout the United States.

According to a 2013 survey by ING Direct USA, a stunning 50 percent of adults who participated in a 401(k) or equivalent retirement plan, such as a 457 or 403(b), left an account at a former employer. ING estimated that amount to be around $1 trillion, as of 2010.[10]

That's a lot of forgotten money!

"Many 401(k) plans are more limited in the number of moves you can make. But generally speaking, the 401(k) rollover is a smart move."

When employees leave a job, they're generally in one of two mindsets: In the better situations, they're off to their next adventure, perhaps retirement or a new job. In those cases, people are often busy, and the thought of moving a 401(k) is the furthest thing from their minds.

In less pleasant situations, people laid off from jobs are busy looking for something new. Here, too, amid more pressing concerns, moving the account from the employer's

[10] ING DIRECT USA Survey: Complexity and Confusion Cause Americans to Leave Big Retirement Money at Past Jobs http://www.prnewswire.com/news-releases/ing-direct-usa-survey-complexity-and-confusion-cause-americans-to-leave-big-retirement-money-at-past-jobs-106442578.html

program and into an individual retirement account is often forgotten.

There are some exceptions, but in most cases, account owners are well advised to move their 401(k) accounts out of a former employer's program.

Sadly, it's not unusual to hear horror stories related to 401(k) rollovers.

We recently began working with a woman who left a job at a major university more than two decades ago. She was entitled to an employer match on the full amount she had saved. (Those sweet deals are still available at universities and some other public-sector employees, believe it or not.)

At the time, she had a different last name than she does today, a not-uncommon situation. When we initiated the process of rolling over her retirement account into an IRA, the university offered to transfer the amount our client had stashed away, but not the match. The university said they could not locate her employee records, and seemed particularly flummoxed by her change in last name.

Well, at our urging, the university dug into the microfiche records and finally located our client. Yes, you read that correctly: microfiche. Sometimes you have to break out the antiquated technologies to get things done!

The moral of this story is: Without some pressure, our client's former employer was only going to transfer half of the money she was owed.

In addition to poor service and the hassle of transferring a long-dormant 401(k), there are other potential drawbacks of leaving it with a former employer.

Poor investment choices: Most 401(k) plans use actively managed funds, which typically carry higher fees than passive or index funds. In addition, the 401(k) choices typically don't include all the asset classes found in a properly diversified portfolio, such as small-cap and emerging-market stocks or short-term, high-quality bonds. By rolling over your employer-sponsored account into an IRA, you have a wider range of investment options, including cheaper funds and those more aligned with your specific risk tolerance and time horizon.

Poor communication from the plan sponsor: Over time, a former employer might be acquired, merge with another firm, change its business structure or go out of business altogether. Any of these changes could affect access to your account. As our client's experience shows, the longer you are away from a job, the more difficult it may be to gain access to your own money. Your former employer is not obligated to keep track of you: If you move away, the company no longer has your address, and you may not receive important updates.

Fewer choices for adding to your account: When you roll over your 401(k), you may add to the account throughout the year, up to the annual contribution limits of $5,500 for those under 50 years old, and $6,500 for those 50 and over. With a 401(k), you're generally limited to contributing when you are paid. Also, with an IRA, you can make changes to the holdings any time you want (although it's not a great idea to trade willy-nilly as the mood strikes — but that's a different topic!). Many 401(k) plans are more limited in the number of moves you can make.

Generally speaking, the 401(k) rollover is a smart move.

There are, however, a few special considerations. For example, if your 401(k) contains your former employer's stock (a risky situation in and of itself), there may be tax considerations of "net unrealized appreciation." These are special cases, and it's best to consult a tax professional or investment adviser if you hold company stock in your retirement account.

Keeping track of your former accounts is a good first step. It's worth that next step of determining whether a rollover or transfer is a better way to proceed.

The worst lies we tell ourselves about retirement

A growing body of research is showing that people have a hard time imagining themselves in the future.

"Salting away money on a regular basis can be life changing."

Harvard psychology professor Daniel Gilbert addressed this issue in his 2006 book, *Stumbling on Happiness*.[11] He expanded the idea in a 2014 TED talk, "The Psychology of Your Future Self."[12]

Discussing his future-self research, Gilbert says, "At every age, from 18 to 68 in our data set, people vastly underestimated how much change they would experience over the next 10 years."

---

[11] Stumbling on Happiness https://www.amazon.com/Stumbling-Happiness-Daniel-Gilbert/dp/1400077427

[12] Dan Gilbert: The Psychology Of Your Future Self: https://www.ted.com/talks/dan_gilbert_you_are_always_changing?language=en

We tend to think we will stay exactly the same as we are today. Of course, a look back at ourselves a decade ago shows how untrue this assumption is, but we persist in believing that our lives won't change anymore going forward.

While it's important to live in the moment and create memorable and meaningful experiences, it's also important to make decisions that are in the best interest of our future selves. In his TED talk, Gilbert says, "At every stage of our lives we make decisions that will profoundly influence the lives of the people we're going to become, and then when we become those people, we're not always thrilled with the decisions we made."

I talk to a lot of people about their plans for retirement. It's difficult to think ahead, even for people who are no longer working but can reasonably expect to live another 25 or even 30 years.

Here are some of the ways people rationalize lack of financial preparedness for a potentially lengthy retirement:

- **I won't live long enough to worry about it.** Forget how long your parents lived; that's not really the best way to guesstimate your own life expectancy. According to recently released data from the Centers for Disease Control and Prevention, a 65-year-old woman in the U.S. has an average life expectancy of 20.5 more years. For a man, it's 17.9 years.[13]

---

[13] Life expectancy in the USA hits a record high http://www.usatoday.com/story/news/nation/2014/10/08/us-life-expectancy-hits-record-high/16874039/

The baby boomers benefit from improvements in medical care, safety technologies and better overall health care habits. You don't see many people smoking anymore, do you?

While genetics plays some role in our life expectancy, many other factors may be more important. So even if Mom or Dad died at a fairly young age, that doesn't necessarily mean it's your destiny.

- **I have a frugal lifestyle, so I'll be OK.** You're off to a good start with this one, but people tend to underestimate how much they'll want and need to spend in retirement.

  You might have heard that familiar refrain that you'll need 70 percent to 80 percent of your current income in retirement. But take this with not just a grain of salt but a full shaker. There's growing evidence that many retirees spend less simply because they don't have the money to afford the lifestyle they enjoyed while working. That may account for much of the spending drop that researchers have found.

  Also, it's very common for healthy and active people to spend more in the first years of retirement. They're finally able to travel and try new hobbies — some of them expensive!

  Finally, even if spending levels out after you've taken that seventh cruise and decided you don't want to deal with travel hassles so often, your health care spending will almost certainly go up as you age.

Don't kid yourself that you can live on next to nothing.

- **Markets are rigged, so there's no point in investing or sticking to a philosophy.**

"The financial media and Wall Street brokers are the only ones profiting when investors become consumed by fear."

We all know the mainstream media loves conflict and drama, and we're apt to view many stories skeptically for that reason. Those fear tactics are also at work in much of the financial media.

Over time, markets go up. There always have been and always will be geopolitical and economic events that roil markets over short and medium time frames. There is no "getting back to normal," and it's not "different this time."

Sure, the particulars may differ, but, in the words of the late Gilda Radner, "It's always something."

Unfortunately, the 24-hour news cycle thrives on conflict and stories designed to scare you and make you nervous. It's easy to get worked up over the Federal Reserve, high-frequency traders,

> Chinese hackers, politicians or any number of perceived threats.
>
> But the media drumbeat only reinforces lizard-brain instincts that served us well in an evolutionary sense, but go against us when it comes to investing for our futures.
>
> The truth is: It's a great time to be an investor. Thirty years ago, people paid high commissions to buy and sell stocks, there was less transparency into what brokers were charging, and mutual funds often came with heavy sales commissions. Today, it's insanely easy to construct a low-cost, diversified portfolio using inexpensive indexed exchange-traded funds (ETFs) or passively managed mutual funds. These instruments were not available a few decades ago.

I'm not being naive. I understand there is always potential for sudden market movements to the downside. But every year, Boston-based research firm DALBAR updates its study that shows investors who make portfolio changes in response to market movements have worse returns than those who simply stuck to their knitting.[14]

In other words, the financial media and Wall Street brokers are the only ones profiting when investors become consumed by fear.

---

[14] http://kickthebucketbook.com/resourses/

Take wishing and hoping out of retirement planning

I recently wrote about getting started on financial goals. One great place to begin is with your 401(k), 403(b), 457 or similar retirement plan offered at your job.

Salting away money on a regular basis can be life changing — and that's no exaggeration. It can be a little painful to set aside part of your salary now, but it's a lot less painful than finding yourself years from now with next-to-nothing in your retirement accounts.

Let's get one thing straight: I often hear people say, "I don't plan to retire because I love my work!"

I understand the sentiment, but it's essentially meaningless. Forget the old idea of retirement as bad clothes, tour buses and shuffleboard. Retirement really means having the resources to do what you want. For many people, that means working at something you enjoy.

But the key phrase is "having the resources."

Contributing to your employer-based retirement account is the first step, but that's not where it ends.

Unfortunately, the actual allocations often get short shrift. That's understandable, because we're left to our own devices when it comes to the investments. It doesn't help that there's plenty of misinformation out there: For example, a popular radio talk-show host advocates growth-stock mutual funds. Well, that's one asset class, and not even one that tends to outperform over time!

Obviously, without knowing your unique situation and your goals, I can't offer specific advice. But I can give you some food for thought.

It's absolutely necessary to have an investment philosophy. Most people are swayed by some pet economic theory or belief that this or that asset class is somehow bound to do well this year. None of those are philosophies; they're just opinions.

Here are the tenets of an investment philosophy: First, markets work. That was true even in 2008, when problems were identified and markets subsequently rebounded. You may not like it, but public markets are pretty efficient, especially over time.

Second, diversification is crucial. But don't confuse "diversification" with "mediocrity." You don't want to spread out investments as if they were bets; instead, you want to take advantage of the higher expected returns of emerging markets, as well as small and value stocks.

Third, risk and return are related. Now, this one may sound obvious, so it deserves a bit of explanation. How many people do you know who have become risk-averse in a post-2008 world, and believe that keeping their money in certificates of deposit or money market accounts is the safest course of action? You may even hold this belief yourself.

But the risk of cash is not what you may think. In this low-interest-rate environment, you are losing money when you don't take any market risk.

On the flip side, making bets on single stocks has its own kind of risk. You're putting too much emphasis on Apple,

Facebook, Twitter or Starbucks. You might think you should be paid more to take on extra risk, but it doesn't work that way, at least not on a consistent basis. You don't see NFL players getting paid more for playing without helmets. Same idea when it comes to your investing. Why would you take unnecessary risks?

The final tent pole of a sound investment philosophy is the structure of the portfolio itself. Awhile back, I spoke to the Rotary Club of Santa Fe about investment philosophies. My talk was titled "Pizza or Broccoli?" It's fun to load up on toppings and have some tasty food, but ultimately, you need a balanced variety of nutrients in your diet.

It's easy to see the parallel to investing, isn't it?

Think carefully when you look at the investments available in your 401(k) or other retirement plan. I frequently assist clients with the allocations in their plans. The choices can be subpar, especially when compared to portfolios constructed by professional money managers, designed to help you achieve specific goals. But if you organize and allocate the best you can, given what's available, you are taking a step in the right direction.

Remember, the majority approach their investing in the vein of the classic Dusty Springfield song, "Wishin' and Hopin.' "

That sounds more like the plan for a weekend excursion to the Bellagio than a strategy for building wealth!

Approach your retirement account with a solid philosophy, rather than with guesses or the economic theory du jour. This will immediately set you apart from others in the crowd, who often doom themselves to mediocre returns.

Invest in a your 401(k), but be wary of fees, mix

I often talk to people about the wisdom of contributing to an employer-sponsored retirement plan, such as a 401(k) or 403(b). It's a great way to build up savings in a relatively painless way.

There's a saying on the website of the American Association of Individual Investors: "Some people spend more time planning a two-week vacation than they do retirement planning."[15]

That saying — attributed to Anonymous — is worth repeating. Investing systematically in one of these plans is a key component of preparing for your non-working years. And don't kid yourself: Even if you love what you do, there will come a time when you will want or need to ease up on the accelerator.

However, there is a dark side of 401(k) plans, and it's important that investors know where they are putting their money.

Don't get me wrong. I'm not trying to dissuade you from contributing. On the contrary, I want you to be fully informed.

Frequently, the mutual fund choices in these vehicles are sub-par, especially when compared with institutional funds available through advisers. Expense ratios can be high, eating away at investor returns.

The numbers are startling. The average actively managed mutual fund — meaning a fund in which a manager is

---

[15] Retirement Planning Myths
http://www.aaii.com/evergreen/article/retirement-planning-myths

making stock and bond picks — has an annual expense of 0.79 percent.[16] When sales charges and other management fees are layered on, fees can run above 5%!

Even for investors who want to understand the numbers, the statements can be daunting for a layperson to understand.

In addition, funds often pay to be made available in a particular plan. It's similar to the way Coca-Cola or Procter & Gamble pay for shelf space at Albertsons. There's nothing illegal about this practice, but it can add to the costs for unwitting investors.

Of course, in a roaring bull market, or even a sleepy and hated bull market, such as the one we experienced in 2013, nobody complains about expensive mutual funds. "My funds did well!" I hear that all the time, as if there were some magic that will continue in perpetuity.

That brings up another problem: More than three quarters of active fund managers fail to consistently beat their benchmark in any given year.

I realize that not everybody is a stock-market geek (I'll cop to being one!), so allow me to dissect the previous paragraph. Active managers are those who — as the name suggests — are actively trading stocks and bonds inside mutual funds. They incur trading fees for moving these investments around. Guess who pays the fee?

Yes, that's a rhetorical question. You know that answer already.

---

[16] 2015 Fee Study: Investors Are Driving Expense Ratios Down http://news.morningstar.com/pdfs/2015_fee_study.pdf

Furthermore, we have decades of market data that clearly show the unpredictability of asset-class returns. In other words, just because U.S. large-cap stocks were a leading asset class one year, they are not somehow destined to perform as well the following year. Investors who owned the S&P 500 in 2013 are understandably happy with their returns. But to assume that an S&P index fund is some kind of lucky rabbit's foot is completely misplaced.

For a fund manager whose benchmark is the S&P 500, 2013 was a jackpot year. But winning streaks end. Fund performance has less to do with manager talent than with normal rotations of sectors and asset classes.

Think of it this way: If all your investments are moving in the same direction at the same time, you have a bet, not an allocation.

So for 401(k) investors, it's imperative to use caution when selecting allocations. I realize that the choices are often limited, but allocating among different asset classes will give you the best opportunity to capture gains where they occur.

This is where individual investors are at a disadvantage. It's not easy to understand the proper weightings within your retirement portfolio. Most people just get exasperated and check a few boxes that sound good. Large-cap U.S.? Sure, that sounds good! I'll take that!

If you have choices, it's better to allocate than to dump everything into one or two asset classes that sound promising or that did well last year.

These are just a few cautionary notes about employer-sponsored plans. It's definitely a good idea to stash money into one of these accounts, but be cognizant about the fees and the mix of assets you're using.

No more excuses: Start saving for retirement

If you think it's tough to save for retirement, you're not alone. In late 2014, Wells Fargo released its Middle-Class Retirement study,[17] and the findings were grim.

Thirty-four percent of working, middle-class adults — defined as those with a median household income of $63,000 — said they are not contributing one red cent into a 401(k), Individual Retirement Account or other savings vehicle.

The study also found that middle-class Americans have saved a median of $20,000 in their retirement accounts. That's down $5,000 from the previous study.

"Some people spend more time planning a two-week vacation than they do retirement planning."
– American Association of Individual Investors

We definitely are battling some headwinds when it comes to saving money, but some of the reasons for not saving are contradictory. For example, people grumble about a poor economy, yet don't hesitate to spend money on things they want.

---

[17] Wells Fargo Survey Finds Saving for Retirement Not Happening for a Third of Middle Class https://www.wellsfargo.com/about/press/2014/middle-class-retirement-saving_1022/

There are plenty of ways you can justify not putting away any money for your later years. I hear a lot of them, but here are some that are particularly egregious.

- **I don't have enough money to save anything.** On the surface, this one actually sounds somewhat reasonable. I actually heard someone make this excuse, then five minutes later tell me about the overseas trip she was taking the following month. It makes me start humming that early '90's song, "Things That Make You Go Hmmm ..."

  Choosing to save for our non-working years means sacrificing today. I don't know what it was like for previous generations — I wasn't around — but it sure seems like the current crop of Americans want what they want, and they want it now.

"The closer you are to retirement, the more crucial it is to get moving. Do something, rather than nothing, and don't just wave the white flag of surrender."

- **Who can save anything in this economy?** This is another excuse that you might find yourself agreeing with. I realize that many people seem to think it's heartless to suggest that it's even possible to thrive and do sound planning in a sub-optimal economy.

The reality is, we never have any guarantees about how the economy will perform. I'm willing to bet many of the people bemoaning the economy now weren't saving much during the boom years of the mid-to-late 1990s. Without a doubt, the downside in this economy is fewer jobs that pay well. The upside? More opportunity than ever before to create our own businesses and opportunities. Not saying it's easy, but more of us today need to be creative about generating income for our golden years.

- **Society will collapse soon and/or the government will just take all my money.** People really do think this way, particularly during an especially contentious Presidential election year.

  Some people I know have been saying things like this for several years, and through presidential administrations of both parties. Not sure when this Armageddon is supposed to occur, but as I tell people: The bigger risk is that the world doesn't end, you live a long life, and you aren't financially prepared for that.

  Sorry, I don't have much sympathy for this brand of fatalistic thinking, and I blame the national news media for stirring up a lot of "the sky is falling" anxiety. Don't let that scare you into complacency when it comes to your retirement savings. Chances are the world won't end next week, we'll muddle through the current malaise, and you'll want to be ready for what emerges on the other side.

- **I don't understand enough about investing.** In my experience, it's almost always women who say this, as an excuse for not saving or for leaving a big pile of money withering away in a money market account. Guys will admit they are not market experts, but they don't usually let that stop them from investing.

You don't need to have to be a market wizard to be a successful investor. In fact, there's really no such thing as a market whiz, given the well-established science of investing.[18]

Get help if you feel unsure. I recommend an approach based on either indexing or simple diversification. In other words, stick to a very simple mix of stock and bond funds, and don't make outsized bets on any particular asset class, or worse, a single stock.

A good starting place is an easy-to-read, short book called *The Investment Answer* by Daniel Goldie and Gordon Murray.[19]

Not everybody wants to learn the intricacies of the stock market, but it literally pays to know a little bit. And you don't need to be good at math to understand the stock market. Investing is more of a social science, not a math exercise. I was a creative writing major in college. Investing is not about math, so don't use that as an excuse either.

---

[18] The Science of Investing https://us.dimensional.com/pdf/science_of_investing_us_2012.pdf

[19] The Investment Answer: https://www.amazon.com/Investment-Answer-Daniel-C-Goldie/dp/B0096ET3S6

Sure, it's wise to start saving in your 20s or 30s, but I suspect for many readers, that train left the station long ago. The closer you are to retirement, the more crucial it is to get moving. Do something, rather than nothing, and don't just wave the white flag of surrender.

After all, those excuses won't keep a roof over your head 15 or 20 years from now, will they?

3

Investing

Waiting For A Crash And Losing Money Along The Way

"Many Americans mistake TV commentators as financial advisers; it's easy to forget they are essentially ad salespeople, with no fiduciary responsibility for viewers' investment portfolios."

I know a guy who has about $300,000 sitting in cash.

That might not sound like much of a problem, but it is. Cash doesn't keep pace with inflation. It may feel safe to be out of the market, but there is a huge opportunity cost.

My acquaintance in California is worried that some catastrophic event, somewhere on the horizon, will tank the markets. Apparently, he believes this event will occur without warning. That never happens; my years of reading stock charts as a market-trading coach taught me that market downturns happen gradually.

(And please don't cite the May 2010 "flash crash" as evidence to the contrary. That was not a market downturn; it was a human or systematic error from which stocks rebounded quickly.)

This acquaintance of mine has been on the sidelines, avoiding the stock and bond markets, for at least two years.

He wants certainty. I wish him luck. We all want that — not just in the market but in our lives. It's much easier to make any kind of decision when we know exactly what the outcome will be.

Unfortunately, there are few situations like that.

In the market, we can sometimes quantify the effects of sitting on the sidelines.

I'll use another example of a new client who came to our offices earlier this year. He exited the stock market in late 2012, when the media were howling about the fiscal cliff scare. That was going to be one of those catastrophic events that was "certain" to cut investors' portfolio value in half, or worse!

We all know how that worked out. Rather than portfolios tanking, the S&P 500 rose a whopping 32 percent in 2013.[20]

So by bailing out of U.S. stocks at the end of 2012, sitting out 2013 and waiting for some devastating event, the fellow who came to our office gave up $115,000.

Part of the problem rests with the financial media. By keeping audiences in a state of panic, they whip up ratings. TV news anchors are not fiduciaries, obligated to do what's in the best interest of their audiences. They are entertainers. Their salary is based on delivering ratings, which, in turn, deliver ad dollars.

Of course, uncertainty can work the other way. People watch the news, get scared (that means the news producers are doing their jobs) and keep their money in cash. It seems "safe." After all, there is always something to worry about.

Even in the past several years, as U.S. markets have been in rally mode, there has been no shortage of uncertainty in the form of geopolitical and economic events, including the U.S. debt ceiling debate, the European debt and worries about China's shift from an export-led economy to something more domestic driven.

How do you balance all this news, all this uncertainty, and make the right portfolio bets?

You probably know what I'm going to say: You don't.

---

[20] Wall Street closes 2013 at records; best year in 16 for S&P, 18 for Dow http://www.cnbc.com/2013/12/31/us-stocks.html

There's an entire industry that's been created around market punditry. It can be terrific entertainment, but it doesn't mean the pundits are correct. I recently interviewed behavioral finance consultant Daniel Crosby, who cited research that showed pundits had no special track record of accurate predictions. The interview appeared on the Forbes.com website. Here's a short excerpt:

> "There is an inverse relationship between self-confidence of predictions and actual predictive accuracy, so many financial talking heads are providing a false sense of security. Real surety is had by taking an appropriately long view of your financial life and relying on a personal expert rather than someone who is trying to craft investment wisdom for the masses."[21]

You might want to read that again.

Rather than relying on predictions for certainty — or the reverse, watching the cavalcade of conflicting pundits on the cable news channels — keep your long-term goals in mind. The talking heads won't provide you with the certainty you are seeking, and they may just steer you in a wrong and very dangerous direction.

Beyond 'Brexit': Stick to your investment plan

In some areas of our lives, we welcome a little excitement and a break from the routine — when it means something fun is happening!

---

[21] Do Your Investing Biases Doom You To Low Returns? http://www.forbes.com/sites/katestalter/2014/05/20/do-your-investing-biases-doom-you-to-low-returns/#405ee3da6ac3

But excitement is not always welcome when it comes to our investments. That's particularly true when a break in the routine means a sharp, sudden decline in portfolio value.

There's no need to rehash all the "Brexit" news here; it's been discussed ad infinitum. At this point, many investors are less concerned about what happened — and why — than about the effects on their own portfolios.

When you see your investments decline because of some news event, there's often a strong temptation to sell your portfolio holdings and park your money in cash until normalcy returns.

This might feel like a prudent response to protect your capital, but it's actually a form of market timing.

I know this isn't easy to hear. I've had people sit in my office and tell me how, in response to various news events, they or their current adviser moved their money into cash.

This was done in an effort to be cautious, but it often backfired.

When speaking with clients, I often use the example of the fiscal cliff scare at the end of 2012. Nobody remembers it anymore — there have been approximately 1,282 new crises du jour since then. To refresh your memory: In late 2012, the national media ran nonstop coverage of the imminent effect of several new laws, all of which would combine to raise taxes and decrease government spending.[22]

The national news channels showed clocks counting down the hours until these laws took effect. They featured a parade of pundits, predicting sudden doom for the U.S. markets and economy.

"If you have an investment plan, designed to generate the return you need to meet your goals, stick to it. Don't be swayed by market "gurus" or scary headlines."

For the TV networks, the fiscal cliff scare — like many other news events — was a godsend: It allowed them to present stories that worried their viewers, which kept them hooked, craving new details. What would Congress do? How bad would the fallout be in the stock market? How much devastation would the fiscal cliff inflict upon the U.S. economy?

Unfortunately, many Americans mistook TV commentators as financial advisers. That's understandable, since the talking heads come across with authority. It's easy to forget they are essentially ad salespeople, with no fiduciary responsibility for viewers' investment portfolios. Many people sold their investments at the end of 2012, with the idea they were "prudently" protecting themselves from the havoc that seemed so certain.

---

[22] Fed chief Yellen's news conference after FOMC meeting http://www.reuters.com/article/us-usa-fed-yellen-highlights-idUSKBN0TZ2UG20151216

But, as it turned out, the pundits were wrong. Congress reached an agreement. The economy, as tracked by the Commerce Department, actually grew in 2013. The S&P 500 index of large U.S. stocks had a total return of 32 percent.

Many — probably most — of the people who bailed out of markets, believing they were protecting themselves, missed out on those whopping gains.

In the meantime, the TV news anchors moved on, focusing their attention on the Boston Marathon bombing, the Cleveland kidnapping case, and the George Zimmerman and Jodi Arias trials. The TV networks weren't responsible for the poor investing decisions their viewers made because they were captivated by headlines.

Which brings us back to Brexit and the markets. Let's get real: Intellectually, we all know that markets ebb and flow. Market downturns flush out excess, and provide opportunities for investors to buy at bargain-basement prices. Since the low in March 2009, the S&P 500 has notched a gain of more than 200 percent — and that's even since the Brexit sell-off.

I like to remind people of that gain for a few reasons:

- Most people are completely unaware that U.S. markets have done so well in the past seven years, because we're inundated with a drumbeat of bad news and dire predictions.
- Although we know intellectually that markets rise and fall, it's tough to stomach the emotional aspects of a roller-coaster ride. When sell-offs occur, our lizard brains override our logical brains

- After a seven-year rally (punctuated by other long-forgotten panic sell-offs, such as one that occurred in the summer of 2011), it would not be surprising to see a correction. Sometimes, an event like Brexit provides a justification for a sell-off that was overdue, with or without that particular development.

Many investors want to know: Is this a repeat of 2008? Is this a "Lehman Brothers moment," when the financial system is on the brink of collapse? The answer to those questions is unequivocally, "No." Brexit, while unexpected, is not the same global systemic risk we saw in 2008. Investors should remember that many pieces of regulation and legislation have been enacted since then to bolster the global banking system and make such meltdowns less likely during periods of stress.

If you have investments, the bottom line is this: There will always be events that roil markets. Normalcy is a myth. By selling out, you risk not keeping pace with inflation. If you plan to get back in, how do you know when so-called calm has returned, and the time is right?

According to a yearly study by Boston-based research firm Dalbar, the average investor misses out on average market returns for one key reason: Trading in and out of the market, in an effort to guess the best times to buy and sell. Don't be that person. If you have an investment plan, designed to generate the return you need to meet your goals, stick to it. Don't be swayed by market "gurus" or scary headlines. In the end, you'll be the one who pays the price.

Keeping the Fed rate increase in perspective

In December 2015, the Federal Reserve raised interest rates for the first time in nine years. In theory, that could have freed the financial magazines and TV shows to move on from speculating about when such a move may occur.

But that would be too easy.

Instead, the rate increase brings up a slew of new avenues ripe for speculation: How far will the Fed go? How will this affect the economy? What does it mean for consumer spending?

A prudent investor will view most market and economic speculation as entertainment, rather than an activity with any real value. However, that doesn't mean we shouldn't put the rate hike in its proper context. While there has been no shortage of panic among investors and armchair economists, there are some important points to keep in mind.

The rate increase was highly anticipated.

The Fed hasn't exactly been shy about telegraphing its intentions, and legions of financial reporters have been busy parsing the words of Fed chief Janet Yellen.

We can clearly see that U.S. stocks, as measured by the Standard & Poor's 500 index, didn't respond by caving after that December 2015 rate hike. True, the Barclays Aggregate Index, which tracks the U.S. investment-grade bond market, took a hit. However, it held up better than it did in the summer of 2013, when bonds took a tumble on fears of an upcoming rate hike.

The 2015 increase was very small.

The Fed's target rate moved from a range of 0 to 0.25 percent, to one of 0.25 percent to 0.50 percent. In the popular imagination, there seemed to be an idea that the increase would be much sharper.

Typically, the Fed raises rates in small increments, although if it sees robust economic improvements, it may implement several small increases in a short period of time, as it last did in 2004, 2005 and 2006, before beginning the reversal process again in 2007, as the economy worsened.

For consumers and businesses, the small increase means borrowing costs are still extremely low by historical standards. In fact, banks, car dealers and other lenders have been known to tout their own low rates as a way of promoting their businesses over others. This tactic may even factor into some companies' marketing plans and may, in some cases, actually benefit consumers.

The Fed raised the rate because its governors took the view that the economy was improving.

Now, this point can be debated among the armchair economists, but data compiled by the Fed show employment on the rise. In the statement issued following the rate hike, Yellen said, "The economic recovery has clearly come a long way, although it is not yet complete." She also said the economy is "performing well and expected to continue to do so." [23]

---

[23] Lesson for Fed: Higher Interest Rates Haven't Been Sticking http://www.wsj.com/articles/lesson-for-fed-higher-interest-rates-havent-been-sticking-1442167699

Yes, many people still have friends, family and acquaintances who are out of work. It's true that economic conditions remain tough for many people. But the Federal Reserve has huge data-gathering and analysis capabilities that are independent of either major party's political agenda.

Whether individual citizens agree or not, the Fed's data do indicate economic improvements. Unemployment has been declining. That may be a tough pill for many to swallow, but it's central to the Fed's decision, and it shows there is some underlying strength to the U.S. economy.

Rates don't always continue rising. The Fed forecast for rates at the end of 2016 indicates a median of 1.25 percent to 1.50 percent. This indicates an expectation that the Fed will raise rates next year by a total of 1 percent, or essentially a quarter-point increase every three months. Some contrarians believe the pace will be slower.

"I'm not singing an endless chorus of *Don't Worry, Be Happy*, but I am saying that your risk profile must be balanced with your need for income, either now or in the future."

Remember, these forecasts are not bound to come true. For starters, market pundits have a terrible track record of divining future events. Also, it's important to note a phenomenon *The Wall Street Journal* reported on in September: In the years since central banks around the world slashed rates in response to the financial crisis, many have tried to raise them again.[24]

However, economic conditions didn't improve enough to justify continued increases. Central banks in Canada, Australia, South Korea, Chile, Israel, Sweden and other countries raised rates, but later lowered them again.

The bottom line is: Keep the Federal Reserve rate increase in perspective. We've gotten accustomed to extremely low rates. Despite the financial media's myopic focus on the Fed's every action, rates remain low. By their very nature, markets and economies are always in flux. That's something investors and consumers can always count on, whether we like it or not.

It might be time to revisit investment decisions

Intellectually, it's easy for most of us to embrace concepts like, "Buy low, sell high" or "Just stay the course."

But when markets begin trading sharply lower, sticking to a preconceived investing plan becomes more difficult. It's tempting to say, "I'm selling everything and getting out." However, that's actually a rash move that could come back to bite you.

I'm not saying you should ignore your feelings about markets. Humans aren't robots, and our emotions play a big role in our finances. The pain of 2008 is fresh on people's minds. It was especially destructive because home values tumbled along with stock values, leaving nowhere to hide.

---

[24] Why We Care More About Losses Than Gains
http://www.npr.org/templates/story/story.php?storyId=240685257

It's understandable that our minds go to that worst-case scenario, imagining that another 2008 could be around the corner. Certainly, there's a constant drumbeat of bad news about China, oil prices, Federal Reserve policies, emerging markets and clever headlines suggesting that another debacle is nigh.

"Balancing our emotions with our investment objectives becomes more important than ever when markets show heavy downside action and the financial media make it sound like the sky is falling."

Nobody has any idea what will happen to markets in the short term, but investors who spent the last seven years waiting for the other shoe to drop certainly missed out on some sizeable returns.

Managing risk is crucial. I'm never one to suggest going all in, willy-nilly, with no strategy. Nor am I singing an endless chorus of "Don't Worry, Be Happy."

But I am saying that your risk profile must be balanced with your need for income, either now or in the future.

People hate losing more than they enjoy winning. This concept is known as the loss-aversion theory.[25] It was first

---

[25] Boys Will Be Boys: Gender, Overconfidence and Common Stock Investment https://faculty.haas.berkeley.edu/odean/papers/gender/BoysWillBeBoys.pdf

demonstrated by economists Daniel Kahneman and the late Amos Tversky at Stanford University.

For investors, loss aversion takes place when people recall portfolio declines more vividly than gains. That can happen even when the gains are greater. The losses weigh more heavily in our minds.

So it's completely understandable that this environment brings back painful memories.

But rather than selling your investments because you feel nervous — or because you are rationalizing what seems "logical," given all the sensationalistic headlines — consider a thorough portfolio review instead.

Is your portfolio constructed from global stocks and bonds, apportioned in a way that makes sense, given your unique combination of goals, time horizon and ability to tolerate market volatility?

If you find yourself worrying about the markets constantly and checking your accounts throughout the day, that usually means your portfolio is too risky for you. It might be time to make some adjustments.

This is true in your 401(k), 403(b), individual retirement account or traditional brokerage account. It's also true in accounts you may have inherited: Just because your parents had a portfolio that was constructed for them in the 1970s, doesn't mean it's the right thing for you in 2016. Don't be sentimental when it comes to your money.

In recent years, as markets rallied, some investors grew comfortable taking more risk, loading up on investments such as emerging-market stocks. Meanwhile, as I noted above, others felt they needed to protect themselves with a large cash hoard.

Most of the time, neither scenario represents the optimal risk-and-return equation that investors need to reach their goals, while simultaneously protecting their assets.

Balancing our emotions with our investment objectives becomes more important than ever when markets show heavy downside action and the financial media make it sound like the sky is falling. Maybe you actually do need more cash than you currently hold, or maybe you could use a down market to buy some investments at bargain prices. Either way, understanding the right balance for you requires more than a guess, based on something in a magazine or on TV.

In recent years, the notion of portfolio return has shifted to one of asset protection, as loss aversion kicks in. That's perfectly normal and understandable in this scenario. It's easy to feel that your risk tolerance is high while markets are trending higher. A correction or sharp volatility brings up more unpleasant emotions that are worth acknowledging.

Are you comfortable that your investment mix is tailored for your specific income needs and stomach for risk? Do you know why each and every stock, bond or fund is in your portfolio? What is each investment's purpose? Can you rest easy at night, secure in the knowledge that your investments are on track to achieve your goals?

If you don't have good answers for these questions, it might be time to revisit your investment decisions.

Following the markets? Keep those emotions in check

It's safe to say that fear affects nearly everyone who has a few bucks stashed away for retirement.

"Advertisers know about our propensity to make emotional decisions, and they create all manner of media to exploit that."

I'm not talking about the kind of fear that causes shortness of breath and a racing heart. I'm referring to the kind where you fret about events far outside your zone of control.

Just the mention of a few can probably make some of you a little anxious. Here are some common things investors worried about in mid-2015: Greece, China, rising interest rates and, in some cases, an underlying fear that something worse than the 2008 financial meltdown is lurking.

Before delving into those market fears, let's take a step back and consider human psychology. A basic fact of life is that humans are emotional creatures. Gender stereotypes aside (way aside), we all make decisions emotionally, not logically. There's plenty of academic research to back this up. At the risk of getting myself in some hot water, I'll even share this: There's a good amount of research indicating that one gender, in particular, is more apt to make emotional decisions. Hint: It's different than the old, tired stereotypes might have you thinking. I'll leave it at that.

(For those of you interested in the research, you can read white papers written by Terrance Odean and Brad Barber, professors at the University of California, Berkeley and

Davis, respectively. The two have teamed up for years to research how factors such as emotion and gender affect investment decisions. [26], [27])

But before any readers become too smug because "the other half" is more inclined to emotional decisions, remember that emotional decision-making is common to all of us. It's the human condition. Our brains are just wired that way. It doesn't mean we shouldn't gather facts and do research. It just means we should be cognizant of what's behind our decision-making processes. I'll come back to that in a minute.

"If you react to every event that the media deems potentially catastrophic, you'll spend your entire day trading your portfolio."

Advertisers know about our propensity to make emotional decisions, and they create all manner of media to exploit that. I don't think I've ever met a person who admits that he or she is affected by advertising. Most people, in my experience, claim they are completely immune to its powers.

---

[26] Trading Is Hazardous to Your Wealth: The Common Stock Investment Performance of Individual Investors http://faculty.haas.berkeley.edu/odean/papers%20current%20versions/individual_investor_performance_final.pdf

[27] Get ready to cash in on the bottom for commodities http://www.marketwatch.com/story/get-ready-to-cash-in-on-the-bottom-for-commodities-2015-07-29

Yet, the emotional appeals work. Your favorite magazines, TV channels and Web pages get a big chunk of revenue, if not all of it, from advertising. If our logical brains ruled the roost, the media landscape would look different in more ways than we can even imagine.

So how does this relate to those feelings of anxiety that many confront when seeing news reports about Greece or the Federal Reserve? It's important to realize that the financial media are not your allies. Why is it that every single one of the financial channels and websites features conflict and drama?

Back when the financial TV networks launched, decades ago, they relied on stock tickers scrolling across the screen and anchors reading dull reports about commodity prices or corporate earnings.

I'm dozing off just thinking about it.

These networks realized that formula wouldn't attract viewers. Today, these same channels thrive on "debate." They get two or more guests, each with an opposing view on the headline du jour, and let them duke it out. If things get too quiet, the anchor will start goading the guests into considering the worst possible outcome of whatever topic is being discussed.

None of this has anything to do with your reasons for investing, but the conflict appeals to the human brain. We like stories. We like tales with winners and losers, and a moral at the end. This dramatic approach to something as important as your finances may be entertaining, but ultimately, it can be damaging.

This tactic is most evident on television, but it's also put to effective use in other media. If you scan the headlines on Yahoo Finance or MarketWatch, you'll see plenty that urge you to take action, based on some forecast or other.

For example, as I'm writing this, daily headlines include, "Get ready to cash in on the bottom for commodities," [28] "Market breadth tells investors to hit pause" [29] and "What Warren Buffett's favorite indicator says about China's stock market." [30]

Implicit in all of those is the notion that investors should shuffle around portfolio holdings because of one development or another. The flaw in that kind of thinking is pretty evident: If you react to every event that the media deems potentially catastrophic, you'll spend your entire day trading your portfolio. For most people, the trading costs and incorrect bets would put a huge dent in their net worth pretty quickly.

Realistically, nobody reacts to all of these headlines. But frequently, when media reports jibe with a person's existing opinion or belief, people will make a move that proves to be detrimental.

---

[28] Stock-market breadth tells investors to hit pause http://www.marketwatch.com/story/stock-market-breadth-tells-investors-to-hit-pause-2015-07-28

[29] What Warren Buffett's favorite indicator says about China's stock market http://fortune.com/2015/07/28/china-stock-market-warren-buffett/

[30] The World Is Not Falling Apart http://www.slate.com/articles/news_and_politics/foreigners/2014/12/the_world_is_not_falling_apart_the_trend_lines_reveal_an_increasingly_peaceful.html

By far, the biggest one I see — and I see this all the time — is people who park a lot of money in cash because they want to protect themselves against some "bad" thing they believe will happen. Unfortunately, that's been a losing strategy in recent years. Over the long haul, it will continue to be, as market history shows.

The financial media aren't responsible for whether or not you outlive your money in retirement. They aren't accountable if you act upon questionable "advice." They are only responsible for garnering ratings, subscriptions and advertising dollars.

Next time you find yourself anxious about some prediction of imminent catastrophe, remind yourself that the network's or website's desired outcome is not the same as yours.

Market decline? If you believe the media, sure

China. Interest rates. Oil prices.

Try rattling off those phrases in a staccato fashion, adding a touch of urgency. You might find that it makes you a little nervous.

If you watch the news, either online or on TV, you've undoubtedly heard some stock market commentators muster up just the right mix of nervous energy and gravitas to catch your attention. They've had plenty of opportunity to test their dramatic reading skills over the past couple of weeks as stocks made a sharp turn in the wrong direction.

Yes, there are geopolitical and economic developments that affect markets. That little voice (either from the TV or in the back of our own minds) likes to tell us, "It's different this time." But guess what? That little voice is a con artist. It's not really different.

I'm not in denial that low interest rates, over an extended period of time, have pumped up market returns. Likewise, I don't deny that an increase in rates will have an effect not only on the stock market, but on the wider economy.

So yes, those are the specifics.

But there has never been a time when the world was entirely calm, nothing threatened the markets, interest rates were set at perfect levels and everybody could happily predict the future.

"I've seen too many people buy into the fear, keep their money tucked away in certificates of deposit or money market accounts, and cause significant damage to their financial situations."

You know what would happen to your portfolio, in those cases, right? It would sit there, like a couch potato watching *Monday Night Football.* What risks would cause people to invest in stocks in such a perfect world? There would be no point.

Obviously, we live in a very imperfect world, with plenty of risks. An investor buys stocks because of the potential reward that goes along with taking some risk.

What's not different this time is that investors have always faced wars, government actions, natural disasters and all the other circumstances that roil markets.

For whatever reason, humans seem to think the era in which they live is just the worst. People see signals that confirm their biases that we live in horrible times, and that reinforces the idea. A paragraph from a Slate.com story that ran on Dec. 22, 2014, sums up the problem:

"News is about things that happen, not things that don't happen. We never see a reporter saying to the camera, 'Here we are, live from a country where a war has not broken out' — or a city that has not been bombed, or a school that has not been shot up. As long as violence has not vanished from the world, there will always be enough incidents to fill the evening news. And since the human mind estimates probability by the ease with which it can recall examples, newsreaders will always perceive that they live in dangerous times. All the more so when billions of smartphones turn a fifth of the world's population into crime reporters and war correspondents."

I'd recommend reading the entire article, *The World Is Not Falling Apart,* by Steven Pinker and Andrew Mack. [31] The authors include some strong data to dissuade any wannabe Chicken Littles.

Why am I such a fan of debunking the notion that the world is a more horrible place than it's ever been? Because I've seen too many people buy into the fear, keep their money

---

[31] The Problem With Financial Literacy Is That It Doesn't Work https://thebillfold.com/the-problem-with-financial-literacy-is-that-it-doesn-t-work-ce79d2800d56#.lnrovci9v

tucked away in certificates of deposit or money market accounts, and cause significant damage to their financial situations.

To compound the problem, plenty of sophisticated-sounding market analysts will pen *Barron*'s columns or appear on CNBC. They will proclaim their reasons why poor conditions are imminent, or are doomed to last. Their arguments often seem intellectually sound, but that's because nobody really bothers to dissect them.

There's a financial adviser in Florida who regularly appears on TV and writes books proclaiming doom and gloom. Before that, he wrote a book saying that the 2000s would be a decade of unprecedented market success. You see how that prediction turned out. In fact, pretty much everything this guy has predicted has been wrong. But the media loves him! He gets interviewed all the time, because, as the excerpt from Pinker and Mack article from Slate points out, negativity sells.

If that guy had a message that everyone should calm down because markets go up over the long haul, he might be on TV once or twice, but the news anchors would certainly debate his premise and probably laugh outright.

When the TV anchors are shrieking about the market decline, the best thing to do is stop listening and go about your business. Markets really do go up, over time, despite all the nasty events that go on in the world. We griped about the fake market hype in the dot.com era, and markets wrung out that excess. Guess what? They rallied back. And rallied back again after 2008. They have a way of doing that, which takes investors by surprise, and illustrates why it's a mistake to try and outguess the market by timing your buys and sells based on world events.

In that sense, I'm willing to say that it's not different this time.

Personal Finance

You Can't Avoid Financial Decisions

"Unfortunately, putting decisions on hold, or worse, trying to ignore them altogether, is a form of decision-making."

Like it or not, decisions about our money affect nearly every aspect of our lives.

Sometimes these decisions aren't so obvious — at least at first glance — and other times they are glaring.

For example, news in late 2015 that Congress was removing the file-and-suspend benefit affects some married couples' retirement-income decisions.

Don't let indecision become your de-facto decision. Your money isn't a separate little area of your life, cordoned off from everything else."

While the change is significant, it does not remove the core benefit that any worker earned over his or her lifetime. In addition, a relatively small number of people actually use file-and-suspend, which has only been around since 2000. It was not a key strategy enshrined in the laws that established Social Security. There's no point rehashing the mechanisms of file-and-suspend here because it will soon be relegated to history.

But these changes are a jarring reminder of the ongoing nature of financial decision-making.

Unfortunately, putting decisions on hold, or worse, trying to ignore them altogether, is a form of decision-making. That unpleasant thing you don't want to think about — like how much you may or may not be saving for your golden years? If you avoid confronting the question, that's a form of decision-making.

Here are some areas where I frequently see people avoid making money decisions:

Social Security: Although file-and-suspend is going away, there are still decisions about spousal benefits, or even waiting and letting one's own benefit grow until age 70. Even without file-and-suspend, many people immediately claimed their own benefit at age 62, without realizing they could collect more if they waited until full retirement age.

This includes people with resources or other income streams that would have allowed them to wait. Now that the laws are changing, it's even more crucial to do a detailed analysis of your Social Security strategy, particularly if you are married, divorced or widowed.

Holding cash: Yes, having too much cash sounds like a wonderful "problem" that most people would volunteer for. But that's not exactly what I'm referring to. I hear from a surprisingly large number of people whose retirement accounts or other brokerage accounts are not invested at all, but parked in money market funds. For some, the cash feels like a "safe" option. However, there's really nothing safe about losing spending power due to inflation, even in small amounts, or facing very real opportunity costs because the money could have been growing, instead of stagnating.

For many people, though, they simply don't know what to do with all the cash. I understand this; the financial media have endless (and reckless) stories about impending doom. They generate clicks and viewership for media companies, but harm investors who decide to do nothing, based on fear-mongering reports.

That annuity you bought: Now, don't get me wrong here. I'm not saying all annuities are necessarily bad. Annuities are simply investment vehicles, structured in various forms. They can be a very effective way for people to "lock up" some money for a few years (and protect it from themselves!) while letting it grow. With fixed annuities, you won't see the complete upside potential that you'd have by simply investing in the stock market, but you are also protected from the complete downside risk of the market. It's a trade-off that many people find worthwhile, if they want to avoid losses and protect their principal, at least with some portion of their money.

Unfortunately, annuities have been painted with a broad brush by some personal-finance gurus on television. Yes, I'm talking about Suze Orman. However, even her advice on this topic has been misinterpreted: She is mainly opposed to variable annuities, and I agree 100 percent. Variable annuities put the account owner at complete stock market risk, with no control over his or her investment options — and there are additional fees, to boot! Buying an annuity can be a very good financial decision, but it has to be evaluated correctly. You must understand exactly what you're buying and why. It's not enough to just reject the idea out of hand, or just sign the dotted line because somebody tells you it's a "great investment."

Life insurance: This is an area where a lack of decision-making can have tragic results. There are far too many stories of a family breadwinner passing away unexpectedly, and the surviving parent and children struggling to make ends meet. Even in a couple without children, if one spouse is a much higher earner, loss of that income stream would be devastating, at a time when survivors are already grieving.

Sure, it's a pain to pay an extra premium every month. All of us already feel nickeled and dimed in all directions. I'm not saying it's easy to set aside some extra bucks for life insurance, but it's one of those decisions that has proven valuable to many households in a time of crisis. Fortunately, term life insurance rates are fairly low, putting it within the reach of many working families and couples.

Don't let indecision become your de-facto decision. Your money isn't a separate little area of your life, cordoned off from everything else. It deserves some real decision-making.

Personal finance: It's not complicated

Let me start with the bad news.

Personal finance is really not very complicated.

Why is that bad news? Well, maybe it's not for you. But for me, who's expected to come up with an erudite column that informs and educates, it means there's not a whole lot to say.

I should probably back up and explain.

"You don't need financial literacy classes to teach you these habits:

- *Live beneath your means.*
- *Save more than you spend.*
- *Stay out of debt."*

Finance can be presented as something insanely complicated, that only people with advanced degrees and elite credentials can comprehend. The Black-Scholes formula, Sortino ratio, risk-free rate of return — those are all minutiae that bog down some individual investors.

But it's not important that someone saving for retirement understand those concepts. They are distractions from the basics of saving and staying out of debt.

Other topics that distract investors include the global crisis du jour. Maybe it's the Japanese stock market, China's economy and the utterances of Fed chief Janet Yellen.

These topics are harder to dismiss, because our instincts tell us that we need to stay "informed," that world events affect our personal economy. Perhaps. But our own decisions about saving and spending have a greater effect. In addition, the media hype events as having the potential to destroy world economies, when, in reality, they're not nearly so devastating.

Remember the panic over Greece? It began in May 2010, and we heard over and over how the "contagion" would spread throughout the world. Greece represents 0.15 percent of world population and has never been a large area of financial exposure for industrialized nations.

In hindsight, we know that the financial media blew it on the call for Greece-instigated mass panic.

But don't worry about the TV reporters. They've moved on to new things to scare you. They won't ever apologize for causing you to mess up your portfolio because of what they said. It reminds me of the old Lily Tomlin joke: "We don't care, we don't have to. We're the phone company."

Substitute "financial media" and you have today's version of that phrase.

The news of the day really has little or no bearing on your long-term financial objectives. If you invest in a globally balanced diversified portfolio, you won't be at the mercy of a crisis in some obscure region.

Even worse, you don't want your portfolio to suffer because of the TV talking heads.

But rather than being informed by the news, most investors just become anxious. Some make really bad mistakes. One fellow I met was panicked by the "fiscal cliff" scare at the end of 2012. He sold a huge chunk of his investments and sat in cash through 2013, while the U.S. stock market rallied 32 percent. So much for expert predictions of a market crash. Our firm calculated that his opportunity cost totaled $115,000.

At the beginning of this chapter, I said I would start with the bad news. I actually have a little more bad news, and it's this: Financial education doesn't matter either.

That might be a shocker, but it's true. Everybody talks about wanting more financial literacy. What does that even mean? Understanding expense ratios of mutual funds? The beta of stocks? Or the dreaded Black-Scholes formula that I mentioned above?

There have been some academic studies recently showing that financial literacy classes have a negligible effect.[32] Often, the subject matter is abstract, so people forget what they've learned because they don't need it immediately. Perhaps even more important, habits have a greater impact on one's financial condition than book learning.

It's pretty basic: Live beneath your means. Save more than you spend. Stay out of debt.

You don't need financial literacy classes to teach you those habits.

---

[32] Clearing the Clutter, and Getting Your House In Order [Podcast] http://brianholmes.com/049/

Waiting to become more knowledgeable is a form of procrastination. If you can keep claiming you don't know anything about money, you've excused yourself from taking any responsibility for your own financial decisions.

So I've given you enough bad news. I'll wrap up with some good news — and it's actually the same bad news I shared in the second paragraph! Personal finance is really not very complicated.

Those of you who are NPR fans may remember Tess Vigeland, who hosted the *Marketplace* show for many years. In a talk last year at the World Domination Summit (yes, that's a real event) in Portland, Ore., she outlined the six tenets of personal finance.

- Don't spend more than you earn.
- Contribute to your 401(k) *at least* to the match.
- Don't carry a balance on your credit card.
- Save for retirement before you save for the kids' college.
- Don't listen to the clowns on CNBC.
- And mamas, don't let your babies grow up to be cowboys ... unless they can find a good health plan.

If you begin with just those basics, you will be off to a very good start.

Clean house: Clear up your financial clutter

The theme of clutter has been popping up in my life recently. Papers were piling up in my home office, and I was avoiding going in there. It was weighing on me.

Then the other night, I happened to listen to a podcast called "Strategic Living" by Brian Holmes. Holmes was talking about the very topic that was bothering me: too much clutter, blocking up my creativity and my thought processes.[33]

I don't know about you, but too much chaos in my surroundings distracts me. It winds up being psychological clutter. I'm not even kidding when I say that I even have trouble sleeping if there are too many piles of paper or just random stuff accumulating around the house.

For the record: I'm not obsessive-compulsive about cleaning, nor am I one of those "Type A" housekeepers. There's usually a low level of clutter that I can tolerate on a day-to-day basis in the interest of moving through life. But I reach a tipping point very quickly where it becomes intolerable.

But Brian's podcast resonated with me.

And of course, it got me thinking about financial clutter. Many times, I've seen people become paralyzed in the face of financial clutter. This is why mass-media personal-finance gurus such as Suze Orman and Dave Ramsey have such appeal; they can give some generic advice that helps spur people into activity.

As a financial adviser and fiduciary, I see on a more granular level the effects of disorganization. There is a quantifiable opportunity cost to financial clutter. For example, I met some people who let a retirement account sit neglected for 20 years. That means they sat through the

---

[33] Survey: How many of us have life insurance? And how many have enough of it?
http://www.bankrate.com/finance/insurance/money-pulse-0715.aspx

2008 market correction without rebalancing or reallocating. It also means they were not allocated strategically to take advantage of the rally in U.S. stocks after 2009. They lost out on tens of thousands of dollars just by being inattentive.

I realize that there's often a level of fear that prevents people from taking actions. What if I really don't want to know how much debt I have? What if I don't want to see how my investments have fared while I neglected them for years? What if I don't want to really see how much I'm spending every month, or face up to the fact that I might actually need life insurance or a will?

I've seen plenty of people in denial about their real situation. I understand that it can be difficult to clean out the financial garage, but the long-term pain can be worse than simply tackling the problem of financial clutter.

As with anything, take it in bite-sized chunks. Here are some easy steps to help you on the path toward financial clarity, rather than burdensome, energy-draining clutter:

- **Gather all your account statements.** These may come from brokerages, banks, old 401(k) accounts, pensions, mortgages and insurance companies. Think hard: Do you have long-forgotten accounts from jobs you held years ago? Even if it's a small amount, put it on your list. The point is to have get a full picture of your financial situation.

- **If you have 401(k)s or other retirement accounts from previous employers, speak with an adviser about consolidating.** The goal is to minimize fees and maximize expected returns. Plenty of people come to my office with old 401(k)s invested haphazardly, with no strategy and using expensive funds, to boot. You don't want your money to evaporate into broker or management fees, so it's worth evaluating your accounts from that aspect alone.

- **Assess your insurance needs.** This can be tricky but worth it. These days, with traditional long-term care policies going the way of the VHS recorder or the rotary phone, baby boomers should investigate other options. More life-insurance policies now carry long-term-care riders. These can also be structured with a death benefit, which allows you to leave something to your heirs if you don't use the long-term-care policy.

Also, see if you are still paying premiums on life insurance you no longer need. A surprising number of people continue making premium payments long after they have retired and their children have left the nest. In many cases, this is money down the drain.

These are just a couple of examples of where an insurance audit could help you save money now or in the future.

I will wager a cup of coffee (my treat) that you'll feel better after starting the financial decluttering process. I've seen firsthand the sense of calm that sets in when people get clarity about their financial futures.

Your financial to-do list before the year ends

If you're like me, you find yourself having a number of conversations in December that include something like this: "Where did the year go?"

Although it's often hard to focus on financial tasks during holiday season, there are actually a few items that deserve your attention before Dec. 31.

Plan your charitable contributions: You have until Dec. 31 to make your charitable donations and claim the deductions on your yearly tax return. Be aware that you need to itemize expenses on a Schedule A to deduct your donations, and the charity must be a recognized 501(c)(3) organization. Most of the time there is no limit on the amount you may deduct, but there are some special rules that apply to vehicle donations. Be sure to document your donations and get receipts.

Remember to take your required distributions: This is an area where many people make a mistake, because the rules are a little convoluted. I'll try to explain it as painlessly as possible: The required minimum distribution is the amount that you must take from qualified retirement plans such as a traditional Individual Retirement Account.

The magic age for the required distributions is 70½. Generally, you have until April 1 of the year following the calendar year in which you turn 70½ to withdraw your first distribution. So if you turned 70½ in a calendar year, you have about four more months to take the distribution and avoid a hefty tax penalty.

However—and here's where the year-end deadline comes in—in subsequent years, you must take your distribution by Dec. 31. If you are a do-it-yourself investor, ask the brokerage that holds your account to help you calculate the distribution. If you work with an adviser, he or she can handle the transaction for you.

Max out IRA contributions: Technically, you have until April 15 of the next calendar year to max out your annual contributions. You might as well use the year-end to figure out how to do that, if you haven't already. For 2017, the maximum contribution for Roth and traditional IRAs is $5,500, or $6,500 if you're 50 and older.

If you're over 70½, you can no longer make regular contributions to a traditional IRA, even if you're still working. However, at any age, you may still contribute to a Roth IRA and make rollover contributions to a Roth or traditional IRA.

Revisit your budget: Remember that? Your well-meaning plan for cutting back on expenses? Believe me, I know how it goes. We have the best intentions for slashing our spending and saving more money, but life happens.

There's no such thing as a perfect month without car or home repairs, veterinary emergencies, unexpected travel or any number of situations that put the kibosh on our best-laid plans. However, the end of the year is a good time to review how things went, and what your expectations for 2015 should be, realistically.

Prepare if you have quarterly estimated taxes due in January: It can seem like adding insult to injury, having to pay taxes just a few weeks after holiday spending. If you are a W-2 employee, and that is your only source of income, your employer withholds taxes from your paycheck, and you don't have to worry about this.

If you are self-employed or have income from freelance work or sources other than a salaried or hourly job, you may need to pay estimated taxes every quarter. Interest income, dividends, stock sales and alimony also fall under the category of income not subject to withholding.

The quarterly estimated taxes for Sept. 1 through Dec. 31 of a calendar year are due on Jan. 15 of the new year.

Drain Flexible Spending Account money. If you still have money set aside in a flexible spending account for health care expenses, spend it before year end. In most cases, if you don't use it, you lose it.

Review your beneficiaries. New child or grandchild, divorce, loss of a loved one? This is a good time of year to make sure your beneficiaries are correct on your retirement plans and insurance policies. I can't emphasize this enough: A friend's mother recently passed away after a sudden illness. This woman had previously named her grandson as a beneficiary on her retirement and brokerage accounts, but never updated these forms to include another grandson who was born later. She certainly intended to do that, but never got around to it.

Harvest tax losses. "Tax-loss harvesting" is a somewhat jargony phrase that the financial-services industry uses. All it means is: Consider selling liquid assets that are now below the cost you paid. The loss can then be deducted from any capital gains incurred this year.

Make an extra mortgage payment. If the payment clears before Dec. 31, it is deductible for the current calendar year.

Defer income. Many small business delay sending invoices until after the new year to keep income for 2015 lower than expected.

Review insurance coverage. If there have been any changes to your financial situation, this is a good time to review coverages and policies.

As you can see, many of the year-end checklist items are really geared toward making your taxes go a bit more smoothly! Others will have the effect of making your life easier and more streamlined. That's really the "secret" to financial planning. We can't anticipate every change that will come down the pike, but by being prepared and having a plan, we can often minimize the times of being in crisis mode.

Expert advice for the gig economy

Whether you are hoping to supplement your full-time income or your retirement income, or launch a brand-new career as a freelancer, there are some high-level financial planning concepts to consider.

That's especially true as the "gig economy" takes hold. These days, more and more people are taking on side jobs such as being an Uber driver or doing freelance writing or graphic-design work

One important note: I'm a financial planner, not an accountant. The two disciplines intersect in places, but each has its own distinct objectives. So I approach any life decision — such as whether or not to pursue freelance income — from the perspective of sketching out your larger goals, rather than first crunching the numbers on your tax returns.

I've been a full-time freelance writer myself, and I'm currently the co-owner of Better Money Decisions, a fee-only financial planning and investment advisory firm.

I continue to combine both careers, which gives me a unique vantage point on the financial dos and don'ts when it comes to hanging out your own shingle.

As a planner, it's my job to learn about what's important to my clients. What are their goals and dreams? What are they hoping to achieve for themselves and their families?

For example, one longtime client with my firm was looking forward to the day when she could take on projects that were most aligned with her values, regardless of how much they paid, or whether they paid at all. With careful financial planning and a solid investment philosophy, she was able to achieve that goal. Today, she is a freelance consultant, spearheading some high-profile not-for-profit projects in New Mexico. She's able to take on labor-of-love projects because she isn't concerned about making enough income to fund her lifestyle. She's been salting away money and investing for the past 10 years with this day in mind.

Begin by asking yourself why you are freelancing. Is this a way to make some extra money on the side? Is it a way of replacing lost income?

If you are in a position to keep working at another job while you launch a freelance career, then by all means do that. It reduces pressure to ramp up your freelance revenue quickly.

In addition, you want to avoid the unpleasant reality of making early withdrawals from your retirement accounts, which can result in costly taxes and penalties. I have an acquaintance who was fed up with his job and decided to jump ship immediately to go solo. That was a mistake. Now he's forced to draw down from retirement accounts, taking the double whammy of taxes and penalties, and robbing himself of the chance to allow these accounts to compound during his working years.

Here are a few planning tips as you launch your freelance career:

Be realistic about business expenses. Does your new gig require any kind of equipment? New computers, cameras, even office equipment?

Will you be meeting with clients in person, or will all your business be done online and by phone? That makes a difference. Even if you will be meeting with local clients, you can save money on fancy office furniture by meeting at their location, or at a coffee shop or restaurant. For most freelancers, renting office space is a complete waste of money.

Do you really need that new iMac when you start out? Or can you make do with your year-old MacBook for a few more months until your revenue streams stabilize?

Be realistic about personal expenses. Maybe it's time to cut back while the new venture finds its legs. Go over your household budget carefully, and see where you can trim some fat. I've had some planning clients insist there is no leeway to slash expenses, but upon a careful look, there is usually some wiggle room.

There are some lifestyle choices here, of course. You often hear advice like, "Cancel the cable TV." But if you're a huge sports fan, you might be miserable without your daily escape to ESPN. So look elsewhere. Maybe it wouldn't be as painful to cook at home more often, and still have access to College Game Day.

Be realistic about ramp-up time. In most cases, freelance income takes some time to accelerate, so don't assume you will immediately replace the income from your job.

Unrealistic expectations could sink your nascent venture before it even sets sail. If you have to take some other part-time work to supplement the freelance income, or even keep your day job and launch your freelance business on the side, that's a better choice than getting behind on the mortgage or borrowing grocery money from your in-laws.

Don't let the health insurance lapse. If you're healthy, it's tempting to say this is an unnecessary expense, even though health insurance is mandated by Federal law. But don't make the mistake of going without. Really, this is non-negotiable, so it's not an item you can cross off your budget.

If you've been on an employer's plan, COBRA coverage can be exorbitant, so you may want to shop around. There are plenty of ways to get group coverage, through alumni associations and even special groups formed just for freelancers. To borrow a phrase from Nike: Just do it.

After you have considered some of the 30,000-foot questions, then you'll want to talk to your CPA about home-office deductions. Make sure your office is dedicated exclusively to your work activities. I heard a story of a freelancer who was storing some cases of soda for the family in his home office. When he was audited and an IRS agent visited, he lost his home-office deduction. Yes, it seems very petty, but best not to take that chance.

Also keep track of your utility bills, as a portion also can be applied to your home-office expenses. Real estate taxes and home repairs may also be taken into account come tax time. Even if all your work isn't done from home, or if you have a full-time job in addition to your freelancing, these deductions can still come into play.

Finally, many people who are accustomed to working for someone else are not in the habit of paying taxes on a quarterly basis. Every month, be sure to set aside some of your earnings to pay your estimated self-employment tax.

You have to consider your leap to freelancing or the gig economy very carefully, but if done right, it can be a very rewarding career, both personally and financially.

Life insurance: Not flashy, but it can pay the bills

I'm fond of ranting about the financial-services industry and the financial media.

Essentially, they are two sides of the same coin. When you pick up a financial magazine or watch one of those financial TV networks, ask yourself: Who pays their bills? It's not the investing public; it's the brokerages and big insurance companies. Whose interests do you think the financial media really want to protect?

The financial-services industry and the financial media often collaborate (knowingly or not) to steer people toward poor financial decisions rather than good ones.

Let's start with the the entire process of financial planning, which usually defaults to the assumption that everyone has a tidy situation, with spare assets to invest, and the ability to get all the life insurance coverage he or she desires.

Doesn't sound like anybody I know, but that's the way the planning industry tends to approach client situations.

The financial media are bad in their own way, trying to convince people that some kind of magical stock trade is the key to a secure life. Typically, these "what-stock-should-you-buy-now" articles and TV segments are created by people with zero experience managing actual client portfolios. They are written to generate viewership or readership, not to help with financial decisions and strategies that have a real impact on people's lives.

Here in the real world, we know that our decisions matter. Those silver-bullet stock trades? They are entertainment, not the reality that pays the bills in retirement or feeds your family if you pass away sooner than expected.

And those picture-perfect models in the financial-services commercials, having such a carefree time? They don't portray most families' reality.

The reality is: We all need to protect ourselves financially.

For example, let's consider life insurance. It's an unglamorous topic (ever notice there are no TV networks dedicated to breathless coverage of the insurance industry?), but insurance is a key component of making better money decisions.

Most people buy life insurance for the first time when they become parents or homeowners. The reasons for it make sense: Nearly all parents would like to provide for their children in the event that the family breadwinner dies early. You don't want your survivors to suffer financially, on top of the emotional suffering, should you pass away unexpectedly. Perhaps you want to be sure your surviving spouse can remain in your home; a mortgage term life insurance policy can address that concern.

However, not everyone is easily insurable. Health issues, such as diabetes, smoking or being overweight can dramatically raise rates, making life insurance out of reach for cash-strapped families.

But financial planning usually involves some kind of sacrifice in the here and now, with the goal of meeting some obligation in the future. The financial-services industry often frames that obligation as "retirement," but it can just as often mean taking steps to provide for your family.

In a 2014 survey, Bankrate.com found that 37 percent of Americans with children under age 18 did not have any life insurance whatsoever.[34] Furthermore, about one-third of the parents who had life insurance were covered for less than $100,000 of protection.

Now, $100,000 does sound like a lot of money, at first. But ask yourself: How long would that really last, if your family needed to replace your earnings, while paying their ongoing expenses and planning for a future without you?

Here's your answer: Not very long, even if your household expenses are bare bones.

So what options do you have if your situation is less than perfect when it comes to making financial-planning decisions for your family?

---

[34] Prosperity Place http://prosperityplace.com/

One option may be high-risk insurance. For example, if you regularly smoke cigarettes, most insurers would classify you as “high risk.” If you used to smoke, but stopped a year ago or more, you can often find a more affordable rate. In some cases, you can even get what’s called a “preferred” rate if you only smoke less than a few times a year.

(Of course, the key is being honest about your habits! It’s not a great idea to say you smoke twice a year, but then something altogether different is revealed in your physical exam.)

Diabetes is another condition deemed “high risk,” yet it affects a growing number of Americans.

According to the American Diabetes Association, 1.4 million Americans are diagnosed with diabetes every year. As of 2012, 29.1 million Americans, or 9.3% of the population, had diabetes. The vast majority have Type 2 diabetes, which is most frequently associated with obesity and other health concerns.

For families whose breadwinner suffers from diabetes or other conditions, such as high blood pressure, high cholesterol or even cancer, there is some good news.

In the past, it was challenging, to say the least, for diabetics to protect their families with life insurance, at least insurance they could find at any kind of affordable rate.

Fortunately, that situation has changed, and several companies have tailored products to meet the needs of the increasing number of people with previously hard-to-insure conditions.

The point is: Don't give up because you believe it's too expensive, or even impossible, to protect your loved ones.

Planning for your family's future is one of the most important financial — and emotional — decisions you will make. It is worth investing some time to protect the things that are important to you, rather than falling prey to the financial industry's views of the "perfect," uncomplicated situation. I don't think I've ever met anybody whose situation is quite that simple. They only seem to reside in TV commercials.

*"Making **better money decisions** means looking beyond a portfolio. It means taking a comprehensive view of your money and your life values."*

Are you making these five common financial mistakes?

For several years, I taught stock-trading seminars for *Investor's Business Daily* in cities around the country. I met plenty of people trading in and out of stocks in an effort to get a return, but I met fewer people who viewed their trading through a lens of financial planning.

One story was particularly heartbreaking. I don't remember where I was — maybe Florida or Texas — it doesn't matter. Before my presentation, I was chatting with some of the attendees. One fellow told me that he was a postal worker and had a daughter starting college within the year, and he had no savings. He asked if he should start trading options to generate the money for tuition.

I could sympathize with this man, but I couldn't endorse his plan. That incident pushed me to learn more about sound financial planning, and to become a licensed adviser.

After being licensed and working as a fiduciary in the industry for a few years, I launched my own company, **Better Money Decisions.** The name of my firm is no accident: Making better money decisions means looking beyond a portfolio. It means taking a comprehensive view of your money and your life values.

But the guy who wanted to trade options to pay tuition is not alone in making investing mistakes. Since I've been in the financial planning world, rather than the stock-trading world, here are some of the most common investing mistakes I've seen.

- **Having too many different stock and bond investments.** It's important to diversify, but diversification must follow an investment philosophy and strategy. What are your investments supposed to do for you? Are you saving for retirement? Are you in retirement? How much money do you have, and how long does it need to last?

  Too often, people just have investments spread out willy nilly, with no underlying investing philosophy. In addition to just a random bunch of stocks and bonds, I see people holding funds at various brokerages and insurance companies. That's not proper diversification; in fact, it can result in higher fees, investing in the same vehicle in more than one account, and further dilutes your ability to have a cohesive investing strategy.

- **Trying to time the market.** This is usually based on something a pundit said on TV or wrote in one of those financial magazines. The financial media's first objective is not to help you; it's to sell advertising and subscriptions.

  At the end of 2012, there was media panic about the fiscal cliff crisis and how that would tank U.S. stock markets. Unfortunately for those pundits, the S&P 500 kept rising. Still, plenty of people believed there would be a significant decline in 2013 and bailed out.

  We know how that worked out: The S&P finished 2013 with a gain of 32 percent. So much for market timing.

- **Continuing to say you don't understand finance.** This one is more common among women, and it's often a stalling tactic. It comes in a lot of flavors, including one of my favorites, "I'm not good with numbers."

- I was an English major. Many top investors and planners had a liberal arts education. Because financial planning is a people-oriented business, not a numbers-oriented business, you're better off with an advisor who has a solid grounding in liberal arts, rather than the art of creating a killer Excel spreadsheet.

  Personal finance is not as complicated as many pundits and advisers like to make it. The only numbers you need to understand are basic, elementary school addition and subtraction, maybe with a little multiplication and division thrown in. Nothing you can't do on your phone.

But I've heard from plenty of women who had bad experiences with financial advisers who spoke in jargon, and left them feeling confused and demoralized. If that happened, it's not your fault. It means you were talking to a bad adviser.

- **Taking the advice of a relative who's vaguely involved with something "financial" or numbers-related.** I know a person who takes planning advice from a son-in-law who is an actuary, and another from a brother who day trades. Neither of those are holistic financial planners — in fact, they're not planners at all.

  I understand the confusion about the financial services industry; my own mother asked if I was a mortgage broker (I'm not). But if you're going to take advice from friends and relatives, be aware that they may have knowledge in one tiny corner of the wide, wide financial world.

- **Giving up.** This is where you just throw your hands in the air and decide it's too complicated, or maybe even that it's too late. I've worked with enough people to know that it may not be too late to shore up your financial position. You might be surprised at what you can do to generate retirement income, even if you have saved relatively little.

Leveraging a lifetime of experience

In the past, the financial planning industry mostly gravitated toward high-net-worth individuals and couples, drawing these clients with images of attractive older people walking on the beach or enjoying their yachts.

But that vision became cringe-worthy after the global financial meltdown in 2008, and people who lost money in the market found themselves having to work longer, or face an underfunded retirement.

In fact, the brokerage firm Charles Schwab even made some commercials in 2010 mocking the idea of a retirement that looked more like Lord and Lady Grantham's on Downton Abbey than the average American's, who might play a little golf now and then.

(Before I go on, I need to point out: It was not a foregone conclusion that U.S. investors had to lose as much as they did. Sadly, most Americans' portfolios were too concentrated in large U.S. companies, which were hit hard between 2000 and 2009. But that's a failure of proper diversification and planning, by and large.)

So what happens when you are eligible for Social Security — or perhaps already taking Social Security — but you're worried about having limited resources as you face 25 or 30 (or more) years in retirement? What can you do?

It's a big question, and one that a lot of folks are asking these days. There is no shortage of data out there showing that the majority of people risk outliving their money in retirement, and not necessarily because they lost it in 2008; many simply failed to save during their working years.

I've written here before that most people reach a day when they just want to stop working and reap the fruits of their labor. But what if there's very little fruit — or none at all?

Luckily, technology and new ways of doing business have opened doors to opportunities that didn't exist even 10 years ago.

My friend Joan Sotkin is a 70-something resident of Santa Fe, New Mexico. She hosts the Prosperity Show podcast (an online radio show) and serves as a holistic business and money coach. [35]

She coaches her older clients to identify areas where they can leverage experience gained over a lifetime.

"People should ask themselves: What kind of experience do they have, from everything they've done and gone through in their lifetime that would serve as good advice for younger people? Older people think their age is a disadvantage, but they have the advantage of advice to give," Sotkin says.

She often recommends consulting for clients of so-called "retirement age." For example, people who have experience in an industry or in a particular functional area, such as sales, can start a business sharing their knowledge with others.

She also suggests packaging knowledge in an e-book or training program that's sold online — and they don't need to be techno-wizards to do that.

"Even if people over 60 feel that they're technologically challenged, they can find others who can do the tasks for them," Sotkin points out. In fact, plenty of millennials (and

---

[35] When to Take Social Security Benefits: Questions to Consider http://www.actuarialfoundation.org/pdf/nasi-final-brief-ss.pdf

even baby boomers) work as freelance tech assistants, helping others navigate all the facets of making products and services available for sale online.

'Life planning' becomes key for boomers

It may seem hard to believe, but in 2016, the oldest baby boomers turned 70.

The impact of the boomer generation has always been staggering, and that will continue to be the case. That generation consists of people born between 1946 and 1964. Nearly a quarter of Americans were born during that era.

Plenty of industries changed because of the boomers: Automakers incorporated features consumers demanded (think cup holders), hotels introduced a greater number of amenities, the health club industry flourished as people sought to remain youthful and energetic for a longer period of time.

But as life expectancies continue to rise, the idea of life planning — as a subset of financial planning, or done in tandem with financial planning — is gaining traction.

The insurance industry has conducted extensive research into U.S. longevity rates. A 65-year-old can reasonably expect to live until his or her mid-80s. The Social Security Administration, which obviously has a huge interest in tracking U.S. longevity and demographic trends, studied the life expectancies of married couples and found a 48 percent chance that one person in a couple will live to age 90. That was expected to rise to 55 percent by 2015.

This type of data is driving the burgeoning "life planning" industry. Retirement is no longer an afterthought, a couple years sitting in the rocking chair after you can no longer work. An image like that is pretty depressing to the boomers, who would rather have new adventures than wither away.

The notion of planning a happy and fulfilling retirement is central to a 2014 book by Barry LaValley and Mark Finke, *So You Think You Are Ready To Retire?* The authors emphasize the need to envision a lengthy retirement phase.

Despite commercials promoting the need for a "number" to achieve a happy retirement, LaValley and Finke say that mental and emotional preparedness is just as important.

"Forget trying to guess what the stock market will do and focus on whether you are on track to achieve the retirement you envision."

It's actually normal — and healthy — to question whether you are prepared for the day you will stop working. In my experience, people are often overconfident about their ability to retire, when, in fact, they don't have the resources to maintain their current lifestyle.

The old model of financial planning as "stock picking" is quickly falling by the wayside. There's increased awareness among the boomers that stock picking and market timing are hobbies encouraged by Wall Street and the financial media, who stand to gain if you watch CNBC all day and obsess about Apple's price or the level of the Dow Jones.

Retirement planning has much more to do with your goals. By the time retirement is in sight, at least in a fuzzy, vague way, most of us instinctively know what kind of lifestyle we desire. I never hear clients talk of yachts and vineyards and all the silly clichés made popular uated by Wall Street brokers.

Instead, people want to spend more time with grandchildren, perhaps do some traveling in the U.S. or overseas, or spend time volunteering for nonprofits or social causes.

The puzzle pieces are not just financial. They are also emotional.

That makes it all the more crucial to fully understand how you want to spend a big chunk of your life — perhaps as much as 30 years — and how you will finance it. It's common for new retirees to spend like drunken sailors as they indulge in travel and adventures they've put off while working and raising families.

You want that phase of life. What's the point of stopping work, or at least reducing your schedule, if you can't enjoy it while you're still healthy?

The best way to achieve the desired outcome, or at least something close, is by being honest with yourself. If you are married, you and your spouse should be on the same page when it comes to questions of retirement goals, both emotional and financial.

Forget trying to guess what the stock market will do and focus on whether you are on track to achieve the retirement you envision. The two are not the same thing, contrary to what CNBC, Barron's, Kiplinger's or *Money*

Magazine want you to think. Remember: They are beholden to the Wall Street brokers who pay big money to advertise. Whose interest do they really have in mind?

For boomers in their early 60s, it's a critical time to be making some important decisions, particularly with regard to Social Security. How does that fit into the overall puzzle? I find that people tend to overestimate or underestimate the significance of this income stream and how to make the best decisions about maximizing its value.

The bottom line: A secure retirement is not about some "magic number," contrary to what the brokers' commercials may say. Financial planning is crucial, but emotional and lifestyle components are equally important, if not more so.

About the Author

You don't need someone to pick stocks or time the market. Those activities, touted non-stop in the financial media, have absolutely nothing to do with your personal financial goals.

That's why Kate Stalter founded **Better Money Decisions**. People face any number of financial decisions these days. But with the financial media encouraging all kinds of bad behavior – like trying to predict market direction or gambling on what the Federal Reserve might do – the odds are stacked against the person just trying to make good financial decisions for the short and long-term.

Before becoming a Series 65-licensed advisor several years ago, Kate wrote in-depth market analysis for Investor's Business Daily. She hosted the Daily Stock Analysis and Market Wrap videos on Investors.com, and taught Investor's Business Daily live seminars throughout the country.

She also hosted the Small Cap Roundup radio show on the Tiger Financial News Network, interviewed hundreds of asset managers for the "Daily Guru" feature on MoneyShow.com, and wrote mutual-fund analyses for Benzinga.com.

She is a contributor to publications including Forbes, US News & World Report, TheStreet and Seeking Alpha. Kate's primary focus is helping clients around the country who face decisions about portfolio allocation, Social Security strategies, insurance needs, estate planning, college funding and all manner of financial questions.

"Although financial decision-making becomes more complicated every year, many people still believe a financial advisor's value comes from stock picking and timing the market. But that's not the value. In fact, that's speculating and gambling – exactly the opposite of good financial decision-making," Kate says.

Kate has a fiduciary duty to put clients first. As her client that means understanding your unique goals and concerns. It means being your coach throughout different market and economic cycles and helping you stay on track, even while the TV anchors and magazine writers tell you the world is coming to an end.

“Investors continue to be hurt because some TV anchor says it’s time to panic. That TV anchor, meanwhile, has no responsibility for your well-being in retirement – or even if you are able to retire,” Kate says.

Kate enjoys helping people make those “peace of mind” financial decisions. For example, the age at which you and your spouse begin taking Social Security can make a tremendous difference in your household income over the next few decades. Nobody wants to leave $100,000 or more on the table – but it happens all the time! This is the kind of situation Kate helps clients avoid, in favor of making better decisions about money!

A graduate of Saint Mary’s College in Notre Dame, Indiana, Kate spends fall Saturdays watching the Fighting Irish on the gridiron. Her MBA alma mater is Northwestern, so she also likes to see the Wildcats win, unless they are playing Notre Dame! She has a houseful of rescued animals, and is trying to get her 5K speed just a tiny bit faster.

Kate Stalter: kate@bettermoneydecisions.com.

(844) 507-0961. www.bettermoneydecisions.com.

Made in United States
North Haven, CT
14 May 2024

52517609R00065